Cambridge Plain Texts

BEN JONSON
THE SAD SHEPHERD

BEN JONSON

The

SAD SHEPHERD

OR

A TALE OF
ROBIN HOOD

CAMBRIDGE
AT THE UNIVERSITY PRESS
1929

CAMBRIDGE UNIVERSITY PRESS
Cambridge, New York, Melbourne, Madrid, Cape Town,
Singapore, São Paulo, Delhi, Mexico City

Cambridge University Press
The Edinburgh Building, Cambridge CB2 8RU, UK

Published in the United States of America by Cambridge University Press, New York

www.cambridge.org
Information on this title: www.cambridge.org/9781107641877

First published 1929
Re-issued 2013

A catalogue record for this publication is available from the British Library

ISBN 978-1-107-64187-7 Paperback

NOTE

BEN JONSON (1572–1637) was equipped by his early
life with unacademic learning and a coarse and shrewd
knowledge of the world. To these two gifts his work
owes its distinctive flavour; and a third gift, genius,
enabled him to turn them to surprising account. His
disgust at the less inspired excesses of Elizabethan
style and his hostility towards the higher flights of
Elizabethan imagination naturally led him, living in
a later and more critical age, to his main literary
task—the foundation of modern English comedy.
But twice at least he suspended his critical severity
to admirable purpose: in that fierce outburst of
passionate disgust and disillusionment, *Volpone*; and
in *The Sad Shepherd*.

The Sad Shepherd is, however, in keeping with
Jonson's other work; and its high place among English pastorals is due to his characteristic qualities—
learning and knowledge of the world. The realistic
details of country life, and especially of hunting, on
the one hand, and the humour and good-nature of
the play, at once robust and chivalrous, on the other,
give life to this story of Robin Hood in spite of the
cramping convention within which it is told. Its
spirit and point of view are not unlike those of *The
Tempest*; the touching, but unsentimental and half
humorous, episode of Amie and Karolin is the Jon-
sonian equivalent of Ferdinand and Miranda, and
Mother Maudlin the witch is a more fragile Caliban.
This impression is strengthened by the opinion of
Dr Greg and others that *The Sad Shepherd* was
written late in Jonson's life.

It appeared for the first time after his death, in the second volume of his works, and with a separate title-page dated 1641. It is not complete; but each act is preceded by a scenario ("The Argument"), and that for the Third Act carries the plot some way further than it goes in the play itself. The text that follows is taken from the First Edition; but the spelling and punctuation have been modernized, misprints corrected, and a few other alterations, which are noted in a list at the end of the book, made. The original stage-directions have been kept, but it has been necessary to supplement them, and in a few places re-arrange them slightly. I have omitted the Argument, except the concluding part of it, which is printed at the end of the text. There is an invaluable critical edition of *The Sad Shepherd* by W. W. Greg (Bang, *Materialien zur Kunde des älteren Englischen Dramas*, Band XI, 1905).

L. J. POTTS

March 1929

THE SAD SHEPHERD

OR

A TALE OF ROBIN HOOD

THE PERSONS OF THE PLAY

Robin Hood.	The chief Woodman, Master of the Feast.
Marian.	His Lady, the Mistress.

Their Family

Friar Tuck.	The Chaplain and Steward.
Little John.	Bow-bearer.
Scarlet. *Scathlock.*	Two Brothers, Huntsmen.
George-a-Greene.	Usher of the Bower.
Much.	*Robin Hood's* Bailiff or Acater.

The Guests invited

Clarion.	The Rich	
Lionel.	The Courteous	
Alken.	The Sage	Shepherds.
Aeglamour.	The Sad	
Karolin (also called *Karol*).	The Kind	
Mellifleur.	The Sweet	
Amie.	The Gentle	Shepherdesses.
Earine.	The Beautiful	

The Troubles unexpected

Maudlin.	The Envious: the Witch of Papplewick.
Douce.	The Proud: her Daughter.
Lorell.	The Rude: a Swineherd, the Witch's Son.
Puck Hairy,	Or *Robin Goodfellow*: their Hind.

[*The Reconciler*

Reuben.   A devout Hermit.]

Woodmen, Servants, &c.

The Scene is *Sherwood,*

consisting of a landscape of forest, hills, valleys, cot-
tages, a castle, a river, pastures, herds, flocks, all full
of country simplicity; Robin Hood's bower, his well,
the witch's dimble, the swineherd's oak, the hermit's
cell.

THE PROLOGUE

He that hath feasted you these forty years,
And fitted fables for your finer ears,
(Although at first he scarce could hit the bore,
Yet you, with patience hearkening more and more,
At length have grown up to him, and made known
The working of his pen is now your own);
He prays you would vouchsafe for your own sake
To hear him this once more, but sit awake.
And, though he now present you with such wool
As from mere English flocks his muse can pull,
He hopes, when it is made up into cloth
Not the most curious head here will be loth
To wear a hood of it, it being a fleece
To match or those of Sicily or Greece.
His scene is Sherwood, and his play a tale
Of Robin Hood's inviting from the vale
Of Belvoir all the shepherds to a feast,
Where by the casual absence of one guest
The mirth is troubled much, and in one man
As much of sadness shown as passion can:
The sad young shepherd, whom we here present,
     [*The sad shepherd passeth silently over the stage.*
Like his woe's figure, dark and discontent
For his lost love, who in the Trent is said
To have miscarried: 'las! what knows the head
Of a calm river whom the feet have drown'd?
Hear what his sorrows are, and if they wound
Your gentle breasts, so that the end crown all
Which in the scope of one day's chance may fall,

Old Trent will send you more such tales as these,
And shall grow young again as one doth please.

   [*Here the Prologue, thinking to end, returns upon a
   new purpose, and speaks on.*

But here's an heresy of late let fall,
That mirth by no means fits a pastoral!
Such say so who can make none, he presumes;
Else there's no scene more properly assumes
The sock. For whence can sport in kind arise
But from the rural routs and families?
Safe on this ground, then, we not fear to-day
To tempt your laughter by our rustic play;
Wherein if we distaste or be cry'd down,
We think we therefore shall not leave the town,
Nor that the fore-wits that would draw the rest
Unto their liking always like the best.
The wise and knowing critic will not say
This worst or better is, before he weigh
Whether every piece be perfect in the kind;
And then, though in themselves he difference find,
Yet, if the place require it where they stood,
The equal fitting makes them equal good.
You shall have love and hate and jealousy,
As well as mirth and rage and melancholy,
Or whatsoever else may either move,
Or stir affections and your likings prove.
But that no style for pastoral should go
Current but what is stamp'd with Ah and Oh,
Who judgeth so may singularly err;
As if all poesy had one character,
In which what were not written were not right;
Or that the man who made such one poor flight

In his whole life had with his winged skill
Advanc'd him upmost on the Muses' hill,
When he like poet yet remains as those
Are painters who can only make a rose.
From such your wits redeem you or your chance,
Lest to a greater height you do advance
Of folly, to contemn those that are known
Artificers, and trust such as are none!

ACT I

Scene I

Aeglamour

Here she was wont to go! and here! and here!
Just where those daisies, pinks, and violets grow.
The world may find the spring by following her;
For other print her airy steps ne'er left;
Her treading would not bend a blade of grass,
Or shake the downy blow-ball from his stalk,
But like the soft west wind she shot along,
And where she went the flowers took thickest root,
As she had sow'd them with her odorous foot.

[*exit.*

Scene II

Marian, Tuck, John, George-a-Greene, Much,
Woodmen, &c.

Mar. Know you or can you guess, my merry men,
What 'tis that keeps your master, Robin Hood,
So long both from his Marian and the wood?
Tuc. Forsooth, madam, he will be here by noon,
And prays it of your bounty as a boon
That you by then have kill'd him venison some,
To feast his jolly friends who hither come
In threaves, to frolick with him and make cheer.
Here's Little John hath harbour'd you a deer,
I see by his tackling.
John.   And a hart of ten
I trow he be, madam, or blame your men;
For by his slot, his entries, and his port,
His frayings, fumets, he doth promise sport

And standing 'fore the dogs; he bears a head
Large and well beam'd, with all rights summ'd and
    spread.
   Mar. Let's rouse him quickly, and lay on the
    hounds.
   John. Scathlock is ready with them on the grounds,
So is his brother Scarlet; now they've found
His lair, they have him sure within the pound.
   Mar. Away, then! when my Robin bids a feast,
'Twere sin in Marian to defraud a guest.
               [exeunt Marian, John, and Woodmen.

Scene III

Tuck, George-a-Greene, Much, &c.

   Tuc. And I, the chaplain, here am left to be
Steward to-day, and charge you all in fee
To don your liveries, see the bower dress'd,
And fit the fine devices for the feast.
          [exeunt all except Tuck, George, and Much.
You, George, must care to make the baldric trim,
And garland that must crown or her or him
Whose flock this year hath brought the earliest lamb.
   Geo. Good Father Tuck, at your commands I am
To cut the table out of the greensward,
Or any other service for my lord;
To carve the guests large seats, and these laid in
With turf as soft and smooth as the mole's skin,
And hang the bulled nosegays 'bove their heads;
The piper's bank, whereon to sit and play;
And a fair dial to mete out the day.
Our master's feast shall want no just delights;
His entertainments must have all the rites.

Muc. Ay, and all choice that plenty can send in:
Bread, wine, acates, fowl, feather, fish or fin
For which my father's nets have swept the Trent.
                    [*Aeglamour falls in with them.*
  Aeg. And have you found her?
  Muc.   Whom?
  Aeg.   My drowned love,
Earine, the sweet Earine,
The bright and beautiful Earine.
Have you not heard of my Earine?
Just by your father's mills—I think I'm right;
Are not you Much, the miller's son?
  Muc.   I am.
  Aeg. And bailiff to brave Robin Hood?
  Muc.   The same.
  Aeg. Close by your father's mills, Earine,
Earine was drown'd (O my Earine!);
Old Maudlin tells me so, and Douce her daughter.
Ha' you swept the river, say you, and not found her?
  Muc. For fowl and fish we have.
  Aeg.   Oh, not for her?
You're goodly friends, right charitable men!
Nay, keep your way and leave me; make your toys,
Your tales, your poesies that you talk'd of, all
Your entertainments; you not injure me,
Only if I may enjoy my cypress wreath,
And you will let me weep ('tis all I ask),
Till I be turn'd to water as was she.
And, troth, what less suit can you grant a man?
  Tuc. His fantasy is hurt; let us now leave him:
The wound is yet too fresh to admit searching.
  Aeg. Searching? where should I search, or on what
    track?

Can my slow drop of tears or this dark shade
About my brows enough describe her loss?
Earine, oh, my Earine's loss!
No, no, no, no! this heart will break first.

   Geo. How will this sad disaster strike the ears
Of bounteous Robin Hood, our gentle master!

   Muc. How will it mar his mirth, abate his feast,
And strike a horror into every guest!

                [*exeunt Tuck, George, and Much.*

   Aeg. If I could knit whole clouds about my
      brows,
And weep like Swithin, or those wat'ry signs,
The Kids, that rise then, and drown all the flocks
Of those rich shepherds dwelling in this vale,
Those careless shepherds that did let her drown,
Then I did something; or could make old Trent,
Drunk with my sorrow, to start out in breaches,
To drown their herds, their cattle, and their corn,
Break down their mills, their dams, o'erturn their weirs,
And see their houses and whole livelihood
Wrought into water with her, all were good;
I'd kiss the torrent and those whirls of Trent
That suck'd her in, my sweet Earine.
When they have cast her body on the shore,
And it comes up, as tainted as themselves,
All pale and bloodless, I will love it still
For all that they can do, and make them mad
To see how I will hug it in mine arms,
And hang upon the looks, dwell on her eyes,
Feed round about her lips, and eat her kisses,
Suck off her drowned flesh; and where's their malice?
Not all their envious sousing can change that.
But I will study some revenge past this:

I pray you give me leave, for I will study;
Though all the bells, pipes, tabors, tambourines ring
That you can plant about me, I will study.

[*sits on a bank.*

Scene IV

To him *Robin Hood*, *Clarion*, *Mellifleur*, *Lionel*, *Amie*,
    Alken, *Tuck*, *Servants*, with music of all sorts.

  Rob. Welcome, bright Clarion, and sweet Melli-
    fleur,
The courteous Lionel, fair Amie, all
My friends and neighbours, to the jolly bower
Of Robin Hood and to the greenwood walks.
Now that the shearing of your sheep is done,
And the wash'd flocks are lighted of their wool,
The smoother ewes are ready to receive
The mounting rams again, and both do feed
As either promis'd to increase your breed
At eaning-time, and bring you lusty twins.
Why should or you or we so much forget
The season in ourselves as not to make
Use of our youth and spirits, to awake
The nimble hornpipe and the tambourine,
And mix our songs and dances in the wood,
And each of us cut down a triumph-bough?
Such were the rites the youthful June allow.

  Cla. They were, gay Robin; but the sourer sort
Of shepherds now disclaim in all such sport,
And say our flocks the while are poorly fed,
When with such vanities the swains are led.

  Tuc. Would they, wise Clarion, were not hurried
    more
With covetise and rage, when to their store

They add the poor man's eanling, and dare sell
Both fleece and carcass, not gi'ing him the fell;
When to one goat they reach that prickly weed
Which maketh all the rest forbear to feed;
Or strew tods' hairs, or with their tails do sweep
The dewy grass, to doff the simpler sheep;
Or dig deep pits their neighbours' neat to vex,
To drown the calves, and crack the heifers' necks;
Or, with pretence of chasing thence the brock,
Send in a cur to worry the whole flock!

   Lio. O friar, those are faults that are not seen;
Ours open and of worst example been.
They call ours pagan pastimes that infect
Our blood with ease, our youth with all neglect,
Our tongues with wantonness, our thoughts with lust;
And what they censure ill all others must.

   Rob. I do not know what their sharp sight may see
Of late, but I should think it still might be,
As 'twas, a happy age, when on the plains
The woodmen met the damsels and the swains,
The neat-herds, ploughmen, and the pipers loud,
And each did dance; some to the kit or crowd,
Some to the bagpipe, some the tabret, mov'd;
And all did either love or were belov'd.

   Lio. The dext'rous shepherd then would try his
       sling,
Then dart his hook at daisies, then would sing;
Sometimes would wrestle.

   Cla.   Ay, and with a lass;
And give her a new garment on the grass
After a course at barley-break or base.

   Lio. And all these deeds were seen without offence
Or the least hazard of their innocence.

Rob. Those charitable times had no mistrust:
Shepherds knew how to love and not to lust.
                    [*exit Tuck and servants*.
  Cla. Each minute that we lose thus, I confess,
Deserves a censure on us more or less,
But that a sadder chance hath given allay
Both to the mirth and music of this day.
Our fairest shepherdess we had of late
Here upon Trent is drown'd, for whom her mate,
Young Aeglamour, a swain who best could tread
Our country dances, and our games did lead,
Lives like the melancholy turtle, drown'd
Deeper in woe than she in water, crown'd
With yew and cypress, and will scarce admit
The physic of our presence to his fit.
  Lio. Sometimes he sits and thinks all day, then
     walks,
Then thinks again and sighs, weeps, laughs, and talks,
And 'twixt his pleasing frenzy and sad grief
Is so distracted as no sought relief
By all our studies can procure his peace.
  Cla. The passion finds in him that large increase
As we doubt hourly we shall lose him too.
  Rob. You should not cross him then, whate'er you
     do:
For fancy stopp'd will soon take fire, and burn
Into an anger, or to a frenzy turn.
  Cla. Nay, so we are advis'd by Alken here,
A good sage shepherd, who, although he wear
An old worn hat and cloak, can tell us more
Than all the forward fry that boast their lore.
  Lio. See, yonder comes the brother of the maid,
Young Karolin! How curious and afraid

He is at once, willing to find him out,
And loth to offend him!
 Alk.   Sure, he's here about.

SCENE V

Robin Hood, Clarion, Mellifleur, Lionel, Amie, Alken,
 Karolin; Aeglamour sitting upon a bank by.

 Cla. See where he sits!
 Aeg.   It will be rare, rare, rare,
An exquisite revenge! But peace, no words,
Not for the fairest fleece of all the flock!
If it be known afore, 'tis all worth nothing.
I'll carve it on the trees and in the turf,
On every greensward and in every path,
Just to the margin of the cruel Trent;
There will I knock the story in the ground
In smooth great pebble, and moss fill it round,
Till the whole country read how she was drown'd,
And with the plenty of salt tears there shed
Quite alter the complexion of the spring.
Or I will get some old old grandam thither,
Whose rigid foot but dipp'd into the water
Shall strike that sharp and sudden cold throughout
As it shall lose all virtue, and those nymphs,
Those treacherous nymphs pull'd in Earine,
Shall stand curl'd up like images of ice,
And never thaw; mark, never! a sharp justice.
Or, stay, a better! When the year's at hottest,
And that the dog-star foams, and the stream boils,
And curls, and works, and swells ready to sparkle,
To fling a fellow with a fever in
To set it all on fire, till it burn

Blue as Scamander 'fore the walls of Troy,
When Vulcan leap'd into him to consume him.
  Rob. A deep-hurt fancy.
  Aeg.   Do you not approve it?
  Rob. Yes, gentle Aeglamour, we all approve,
And come to gratulate your just revenge;
Which since it is so perfect, we now hope
You'll leave all care thereof, and mix with us
In all the proffer'd solace of the spring.
  Aeg. A spring, now she is dead! Of what? Of thorns,
Briars and brambles, thistles, burs, and docks,
Cold hemlock, yew, the mandrake, or the box?
These may grow still, but what can spring beside?
Did not the whole earth sicken when she died?
As if there since did fall one drop of dew
But what was wept for her; or any stalk
Did bear a flower, or any branch a bloom,
After her wreath was made! In faith, in faith,
You do not fair to put these things upon me,
Which can in no sort be: Earine,
Who had her very being and her name
With the first knots or buddings of the spring,
Born with the primrose and the violet
Or earliest roses blown; when Cupid smil'd,
And Venus led the Graces out to dance,
And all the flowers and sweets in Nature's lap
Leap'd out, and made their solemn conjuration
To last but while she liv'd! Do not I know
How the vale wither'd the same day; how Dove,
Dean, Eye, and Erewash, Idle, Smite, and Soar
Each broke his urn, and twenty waters more
That swell'd proud Trent shrunk themselves dry; that
      since

No sun or moon or other cheerful star
Look'd out of heaven, but all the cope was dark
As it were hung so for her exequies?
And not a voice or sound to ring her knell
But of that dismal pair, the screeching owl
And buzzing hornet! Hark, hark, hark, the foul
Bird, how she flutters with her wicker wings!
Peace, you shall hear her screech.
 Cla.   Good Karolin, sing;
Help to divert this fancy.
 Kar.   All I can.

The Song,

which while Karolin sings Aeglamour reads.

Though I am young, and cannot tell
 Either what death or love is well,
Yet I have heard they both bear darts,
 And both do aim at human hearts;
And then again I have been told
 Love wounds with heat, as death with cold;
So that I fear they do but bring
 Extremes to touch and mean one thing.

As in a ruin we it call
 One thing to be blown up or fall,
Or to our end like way may have
 By a flash of lightning or a wave;
So love's inflamed shaft or brand
 May kill as soon as death's cold hand,
Except love's fires the virtue have
 To fright the frost out of the grave.

Aeg. Do you think so? Are you in that good
    heresy—
I mean opinion? If you be, say nothing:
I'll study it as a new philosophy,
But by myself alone; now you shall leave me.
Some of these nymphs here will reward you: this,
This pretty maid, although but with a kiss.
               [He forces Amie to kiss him.
Liv'd my Earine, you should have twenty;
For every line here one I would allow them
From mine own store, the treasure I had in her:
Now I am poor as you.
  Kar.   And I a wretch.
  Cla. Yet keep an eye upon him, Karolin.
    [Aeglamour goes out, and Karolin follows him
  Mel. Alas, that ever such a generous spirit
As Aeglamour's should sink by such a loss!
  Cla. The truest lovers are least fortunate:
Look all their lives and legends, what they call
The lovers' scriptures, Heliodore's, or Tatii,
Longi, Eustathii, Prodomi; you'll find it.
What think you, father?
  Alk.   I have known some few,
And read of more, who've had their dose, and deep,
Of these sharp bitter-sweets.
  Lio.   But what is this
To jolly Robin, who the story is
Of all beatitude in love?
  Cla.   And told
Here every day with wonder on the wold.
  Lio. And with fame's voice.
  Alk.   Save that some folk delight
To blend all good of others with some spite.

Cla. He and his Marian are the sum and talk
Of all that breathe here, in the greenwood walk.
   Mel. Or Belvoir vale.
   Lio.   The turtles of the wood.
   Cla. The billing pair.
   Alk.   And so are understood
For simple loves, and sampled lives beside.
   Mel. Faith, so much virtue should not be envy'd.
   Alk. Better be so than pitied, Mellifleur:
For gainst all envy virtue is a cure,
But wretched pity ever calls on scorns.
The deer's brought home! I hear it by their horns.

Scene VI

To *Robin*, &c. *Marian, John, Scarlet, Scathlock.*

   Rob. My Marian, and my mistress!
   Mar.   My lov'd Robin!
   Mel. The moon's at full: the happy pair are met.
   Mar. How hath this morning paid me for my
      rising,
First with my sports, but most with meeting you!
I did not half so well reward my hounds
As she hath me to-day, although I gave them
All the sweet morsels, caul, tongue, ears, and doucets.
   Rob. What, and the inch-pin?
   Mar.   Yes.
   Rob.   Your sports then pleas'd you?
   Mar. You are a wanton.
   Rob.   One I do confess
I wanted till you came; but now I have you,
I'll grow to your embraces, till two souls,

Distilled into kisses through our lips,
Do make one spirit of love.
  Mar.   Oh, Robin! Robin!
  Rob. Breathe, breathe awhile: what says my gentle
   Marian?
  Mar. Could you so long be absent?
  Rob.   What, a week?
Was that so long?
  Mar.   How long are lovers' weeks,
Do you think, Robin, when they are asunder?
Are they not prisoners' years?
  Rob.   To some they seem so;
But, being met again, they're schoolboys' hours.
  Mar. That have got leave to play; and so we use
   them.
  Rob. Had you good sport i' your chase to-day?
  John.   Oh, prime!
  Mar. A lusty stag.
  Rob.   And hunted ye at force?
  Mar. In a full cry.
  John.   And never hunted change.
  Rob. You had staunch hounds, then.
  Mar.   Old and sure: I love
No young rash dogs, no more than changing friends.
  Rob. What relays set you?
  John.   None at all; we laid not
In one fresh dog.
  Rob.   He stood not long, then?
  Scar.   Yes,
Five hours and more. A great large deer!
  Rob.   What head?
  John. Forked. A hart of ten.
  Mar.   He is good venison,

According to the season in the blood,
I'll promise all your friends, for whom he fell.
   John. But at his fall there happ'd a chance—
   Mar.   Worth mark.
   Rob. Ay, what was that, sweet Marian?
                                   [*He kisses her.*
   Mar.   You'll not hear?
   Rob. I love these interruptions in a story;
                              [*He kisses her again.*
They make it sweeter.
   Mar.   You do know, as soon
As the assay is taken—
                              [*He kisses her again.*
   Rob.   On, my Marian!
I did but take the assay.
   Mar.   You stop one's mouth
And yet you bid them speak—when the arber's made—
   Rob. Pull'd down and paunch turn'd out—
   Mar.   He that undoes him
Doth cleave the brisket-bone, upon the spoon
Of which a little gristle grows: you call it—
   Rob. The raven's bone.
   Mar.   Now, o'er head sat a raven,
On a sere bough, a grown great bird, and hoarse,
Who all the while the deer was breaking up
So croak'd and cry'd for it as all the huntsmen,
Especially old Scathlock, thought it ominous;
Swore it was Mother Maudlin, whom he met
At the day-dawn just as he rous'd the deer
Out of his lair; but we made shift to run him
Off his four legs, and sunk him ere we left.
Is the deer come?
   Scat.   He lies within o' the dresser.

Mar. Will you go see him, Mellifleur?
Mel.   I attend you.
Mar. Come, Amie, you'll go with us?
Am.   I am not well.
Lio. She's sick of the young shepherd that bekiss'd
    her.
Mar. Friend, cheer your friends up; we will eat
    him merrily.
        [exeunt Marian, Mellifleur, and Amie.
Alk. Saw you the raven, friend?
Scat.   Ay, quha suld let me?
I suld be afraid o' you, sir, suld I?
Cla.   Huntsman,
A dram more of civility would not hurt you.
Rob. Nay, you must give them all their rudenesses;
They are not else themselves, without their language.
Alk. And what do you think of her?
Scat.   As of a witch.
They call her a wise woman, but I think her
An arrant witch.
Cla.   And wherefore think you so?
Scat. Because I saw her since, broiling the bone
Was cast her at the quarry.
Alk.   Where saw you her?
Scat. I' the chimley nuik within: she's there now.
Rob.   Marian!

SCENE VII

To them *Maudlin*, in *Marian's* shape.

Rob. Your hunt holds in his tale still, and tells
  more.

Maud. My hunt? what tale?

Rob.   How! cloudy, Marian?
What look is this?

Maud.   A fit one, sir, for you.
Hand off, rude ranger! [*To Scathlock.*] Sirrah, get
  you in,
And bear the venison hence: it is too good
For these coarse rustic mouths, that cannot open
Or spend a thank for't. A starv'd mutton's carcase
Would better fit their palates. See it carried
To Mother Maudlin's, whom you call the witch, sir.
Tell her I sent it to make merry with;
She'll turn us thanks at least. Why stand'st thou,
  groom?   [*exit Scathlock.*

Rob. I wonder he can move, that he's not fix'd,
If that his feeling be the same with mine
I dare not trust the faith of mine own senses;
I fear mine eyes and ears; this is not Marian,
Nor am I Robin Hood. I pray you, ask her,
Ask her, good shepherds, ask her all for me,
Or rather ask yourselves if she be she,
Or I be I.

Maud.   Yes, and you are the spy,
And the spied spy, that watch upon my walks,
To inform what deer I kill, or give away,
Where, when, to whom. But spy your worst, good spy!
I will dispose of this where least you like.

Fall to your cheese-cakes, curds, and clotted cream,
Your fools, your flawns, and of ale a stream
To wash it from your livers; strain ewe's milk
Into your cider sillabubs, and be drunk
To him whose fleece hath brought the earliest lamb
This year, and wears the baldric at your board,
Where you may all go whistle, and record
This in your dance, and foot it lustily!
[She leaves them.

  Rob. I pray you, friends, do you hear and see as
    I do?
Did the same accents strike your ears, and objects
Your eyes, as mine?
  Alk.   We taste the same reproaches.
  Lio. Have seen the changes.
  Rob.   Are we not all chang'd,
Transformed from ourselves?
  Lio.   I do not know;
The best is silence.
  Alk.   And to await the issue.
  Rob. The dead or lazy wait for't! I will find it.
[exeunt.

ACT II

SCENE I

Maudlin, Douce.

   Maud. Have I not left 'em in a brave confusion,
Amaz'd their expectation, got their venison,
Troubled their mirth and meeting, made them doubtful
And jealous of each other, all distracted,
And in the close uncertain of themselves?
This can your mother do, my dainty Douce;
Take any shape upon her, and delude
The senses best acquainted with their owners.
The jolly Robin, who hath bid this feast,
And made this solemn invitation,
I ha' possessed so with sick dislikes
Of his own Marian, that, albe he know her
As doth the vaulting hart his venting hind,
He ne'er fra' hence sall neis her i' the wind
To his first liking.
   Dou.   Did you so disstate him?
   Maud. As far as her proud scorning him could bate
Or blunt the edge of any lover's temper.
   Dou. But were ye like her, mother?
   Maud.   So like, Douce,
As, had she seen me hersell, hersell had doubted
Whether had been the liker of the twa.
This can your mother do. I tell you, daughter,
I ha' but dight ye yet i' the out-dress
And parel of Earine; but this raiment,
These very weeds, sall make ye as, but coming
In view or ken of Aeglamour, your form
Shall show too slippery to be look'd upon,

And all the forest swear you to be she.
They shall rin after ye, and wage the odds
Upon their own deceived sights ye are her,
Whilst she (poor lass) is stock'd up in a tree,
Your brother Lorell's prize: for so my largess
Hath lotted her, to be your brother's mistress
Gif she can be reclaim'd; gif not, his prey.
And here he comes, new claithed like a prince
Of swineherds; sic he seems, dight i' the spoils
Of those he feeds, a mighty lord of swine!
He's comand now to woo. Let's step aside,
And hear his love-craft: see, he opes the door,
And takes her by the hand, and helps her forth!
This is true courtship, and becomes his ray.

Scene II

Lorell, Earine, Maudlin, Douce.

Lor. Ye kind to others, but ye coy to me,
Deft mistress, whiter than the cheese new press'd,
Smoother than cream, and softer than the curds,
Why start ye from me ere ye hear me tell
My wooing errand, and what rents I have,
Large herds and pastures, swine and kye mine own?
And though my nase be camus'd, my lips thick,
And my chin bristled, Pan, great Pan, was such,
Who was the chief of herdsmen, and our sire.
I am na fay, na incubus, na changelin',
But a good man that lives o' my awn gear.
This house, these grounds, this stock, is all mine awn.
  Ear. How better 'twere to me this were not known!
  Maud. She likes it not; but it is boasted well.
  Lor. An hundred udders for the pail I have

That gi' me milk and curds, that make me cheese
To cloy the merkats; twenty swarm of bees,
Whilk all the summer hum about the hive,
And bring me wax and honey in belive;
An aged oak, the king of all the field,
With a broad beech there grows afore my dur,
That mickle mast unto the ferm doth yield;
A chestnut, whilk hath larded mony a swine,
Whose skins I wear to fend me fra' the cold;
A poplar green and with a kerved seat,
Under whose shade I solace in the heat,
And thence can see gang out and in my neat.
Twa trilland brooks, each from his spring doth meet,
And make a river to refresh my feet,
In which each morning ere the sun doth rise
I look myself, and clear my pleasant eyes,
Before I pipe; for therein I have skill
'Bove other swineherds. Bid me, and I will
Straight play to you, and make you melody.
   Ear. By no means. Ah, to me all minstrelsy
Is irksome, as are you.
   Lor.   Why scorn you me?
Because I am a herdsman, and feed swine?
                  [*He draws out other presents.*
I am a lord of other gear: this fine
Smooth bauson's cub, the young grice of a gray;
Twa tiny urshins, and this ferret gay.
   Ear. Out on them! what are these?
   Lor.   I give 'em ye
As presents, mistress.
   Ear.   Oh, the fiend and thee!
Gar take them hence; they fewmand all the claithes,
And prick my coats; hence with 'em, limmer lown,

Thy vermin and thyself—thyself art one.
Ay, lock me up. All's well when thou art gone.

> [*exit Earine.*

Scene III

Lorell, Maudlin, Douce.

Lor. Did you hear this? She wish'd me at the fiend,
With all my presents.

    Maud.   A tu lucky end
She wishend thee, foul limmer, dritty lown!
Gud faith, it duills me that I am thy mother;
And see, thy sister scorns thee for her brother!
Thou woo thy love, thy mistress, with twa hedgehogs,
A stinkand brock, a polecat! Out, thou howlet!
Thou should'st ha' given her a madge-owl, and then
Thou hadst made a present o' thyself, Owl-spiegle!

    Dou. Why, mother, I have heard ye bid to give,
And often, as the cause calls.

    Maud.   I know well
It is a witty part sometimes to give;
But what, to wham? no monsters, nor to maidens.
He suld present them with mair pleasand things,
Things natural, and what all women covet
To see: the common parent of us all,
Which maids will twire at 'tween their fingers, thus!—
With which his sire gat him; he's get another,
And so beget posterity upon her.
This he should do. False geldin', gang thy gait,
And du thy turns betimes; or I's gar take
Thy new breeks fra' thee and thy dublet tu.
The tailor and the souter sall undu
All they ha' made, except thou manlier woo.

> [*Lorell goes out.*

Dou. Gud mother, gif you chide him, he'll du wairse.
   Maud. Hang him! I geif him to the devil's eirse.
But ye, my Douce, I charge ye show yoursell
Tu all the shepherds bauldly; gang amang 'em,
Be mickle i' their eye, frequent and fugeand;
And, gif they ask ye of Earine,
Or of these claithes, say that I ga' 'em ye,
And say no more. I ha' that wark in hand,
That web upo' the lume, sall gar 'em think
By then, they feelin' their own frights and fears,
I's pu' the world or nature 'bout their ears.
But hear ye, Douce! because ye may meet me
In mony shapes tu-day, where'er you spy
This browdred belt with characters, 'tis I.
A gipsen lady and a right beldame
Wrought it by moonshine for me and starlight
Upo' your grannam's grave, that very night
We earth'd her in the shades, when our dame Hecat
Made it her gang-night over the kirkyard,
With all the barkand parish-tykes set at her;
While I sat whirland of my brazen spindle:
At every twisted thread my rock let fly
Unto the sewster, who did sit me nigh,
Under the town turnpike; which ran each spell
She stitched in the work, and knit it well.
See ye take tent to this, and ken your mother.
                            [exeunt.

Scene IV

Marian, Mellifleur, Amie.

  Mar. How do you, sweet Amie, yet?
    Mel.   She cannot tell·
If she could sleep, she says she should do well.

She feels a hurt; but where, she cannot show
Any least sign that she is hurt or no.
Her pain's not doubtful to her, but the seat
Of her pain is. Her thoughts too work and beat,
Oppress'd with cares; but why, she cannot say.
All matter of her care is quite away.

   Mar. Hath any vermin broke into your fold,
Or any rot seiz'd on your flock, or cold?
Or hath your fighting ram burst his hard horn,
Or any ewe her fleece or bag hath torn,
My gentle Amie?

   Am.   Marian, none of these.

   Mar. Have you been stung by wasps or angry bees,
Or ras'd with some rude bramble or rough briar?

   Am. No, Marian; my disease is somewhat nigher.
I weep and boil away myself in tears,
And then my panting heart would dry those fears.
I burn, though all the forest lend a shade;
And freeze, though the whole wood one fire were made.

   Mar. Alas!

   Am. I often have been torn with thorn and briar
Both in the leg and foot and somewhat higher,
Yet gave not then such fearful shrieks as these.
Ah!
I often have been stung too with curst bees,
Yet not remember that I then did quit
Either my company or mirth for it.
Ah!
And therefore what it is that I feel now,
And know no cause of it, nor where, nor how
It enter'd in me, nor least print can see,
I feel afflicts me more than briar or bee.
Oh!

How often, when the sun, heaven's brightest birth,
Hath with his burning fervour cleft the earth,
Under a spreading elm or oak, hard by
A cool clear fountain, could I sleeping lie,
Safe from the heat! but now no shady tree
Nor purling brook can my refreshing be.
Oft, when the meadows were grown rough with
         frost,
The rivers ice-bound, and their currents lost,
My thick warm fleece I wore was my defence,
Or large good fires I made drave winter thence.
But now my whole flock's fells, nor this thick grove
Enflam'd to ashes, can my cold remove.
It is a cold and heat that doth outgo
All sense of winters and of summers so.

SCENE V

To them *Robin Hood, Clarion, Lionel, Alken.*

   Rob. Oh, are you here, my mistress?
   Mar. [*She, seeing him, runs to embrace him.*] Ay,
      my love!
Where should I be but in my Robin's arms,
The sphere which I delight in so to move?
   Rob. [*He puts her back.*] What! the rude ranger,
      and spied spy? Hand off!
You are for no such rustics.
   Mar.   What means this,
Thrice worthy Clarion, or wise Alken, know ye?
   Rob. 'Las no, not they! A poor starv'd mutton's
      carcase
Would better fit their palates than your venison!

Mar. What riddle's this? Unfold yourself, dear
    Robin!

Rob. You have not sent your venison hence by
    Scathlock
To Mother Maudlin?

Mar.   I to Mother Maudlin?
Will Scathlock say so?

Rob.   Nay, we will all swear so:
For all did hear it when you gave the charge so,
Both Clarion, Alken, Lionel, myself.

Mar. Good honest shepherds, masters of your
    flocks,
Simple and virtuous men, no others' hirelings,
Be not you made to speak against your conscience
That which may soil the truth! I send the venison
Away, by Scathlock, and to Mother Maudlin?
I came to show it here to Mellifleur,
I do confess, but Amie's falling ill
Did put us off it; since, we employ'd ourselves
In comforting of her. [*Scathlock enters.*] Oh, here he
    is!
Did I, sir, bid you bear away the venison
To Mother Maudlin?

Scat.   Ay, gud faith, madam,
Did you, and I ha' done it.

Mar.   What ha' you done?

Scat. Obey'd your hests, madam; done your com-
    mands.

Mar. Done my commands, dull groom? Fetch it
    again,
Or kennel with the hounds. Are these the arts,
Robin, you rede your rude ones of the wood,
To countenance your quarrels and mistakings,

Or are the sports to entertain your friends
Those formed jealousies? Ask of Mellifleur
If I were ever from her here or Amie
Since I came in with them, or saw this Scathlock
Since I related to you his tale o' the raven.
   Scat. Ay, say you so?   [*Scathlock goes out.*
   Mel.   She never left my side
Since I came in here, nor I hers.
   Cla.   This's strange!
Our best of senses were deceiv'd, our eyes, then.
   Lio. And ears too.
   Mar.   What you have concluded on
Make good, I pray you.
   Am.   Oh, my heart, my heart!
   Mar. My heart it is is wounded, pretty Amie;
Report not you your griefs; I'll tell for all.
   Mel. Somebody is to blame; there is a fault.
   Mar. Try if you can take rest. A little slumber
Will much refresh you, Amie.
   Alk.   What's her grief?
   Mar. She does not know, and therein she is happy.

Scene VI

To them *John, Maudlin.*

   John. Here's Mother Maudlin come to give you
      thanks,
Madam, for some late gift she hath receiv'd,
Which she's not worthy of, she says; but cracks
And wonders of it, hops about the house
Transported with the joy.   [*exit John.*
   Maud. [*She danceth.*] Send me a stag,
A whole stag, madam, and so fat a deer,

So fairly hunted, and at such a time too,
When all your friends were here!
   Rob.   Do you mark this, Clarion?
Her own acknowledgment!
   Maud.   'Twas such a bounty
And honour done to your poor bedeswoman,
I know not how to owe it, but to thank you;
And that I come to du. I shall go round,
And giddy, with the toy of the good turn.
                      [*She turns round till she falls.*
        Look out, look out, gay folk about,
        And see me spin; the ring I'm in
        Of mirth and glee, with thanks for fee
        The heart puts on, for th' venison
        My lady sent, which shall be spent
        In draughts of wine, to fume up fine
        Into the brain, and down again
        Fall in a swown upo' the groun'.
   Rob. Look to her! She is mad.
   Maud.   My son hath sent you
A pot of strawberries gather'd in the wood,
His hogs would else have rooted up or trod;
With a choice dish of wildings here, to scald
And mingle with your cream.
   Mar.   Thank you, good Maudlin,
And thank your son. Go bear them in to Much,
Th' acater; let him thank her. Surely, mother,
You were mistaken, or my woodmen more,
Or most myself, to send you all our store
Of venison hunted for ourselves this day!
You will not take it, mother, I dare say,
If we'd entreat you, when you know our guests.
Red deer is head still of the forest feasts.

Maud. But I knaw ye, a right free-hearted lady,
Can spare it out of superfluity.
I have departit it 'mong my poor neighbours,
To speak your largess.
  Mar.   I not gave it, mother;
You have done wrong, then. I know how to place
My gifts, and where, and when, to find my seasons
To give, not throw away, my courtesies.
  Maud. Count you this thrown away?
  Mar.   What's ravish'd from me
I count it worse, as stol'n; I lose my thanks.
But leave this quest: they fit not you nor me,
Maudlin, contentions of this quality.
[*Scathlock enters.*] How now?
  Scat. Your stag's return'd upon my shoulders:
He has found his way into the kitchen again
With his two legs, if now your cook can dress him.
'Slid, I thought the swineherd would ha' beat me,
He looks so big, the sturdy carle, lewd Lorell!
  Mar. There, Scathlock, for thy pains; thou hast
    deserv'd it.   [*Marian gives him gold.*
  Maud. Do you give a thing, and take a thing,
    madam?
  Mar. No, Maudlin, you had imparted to your
    neighbours,
As much good do't them! I have done no wrong.

·The First Charm.

  Maud. The spit stand still, no broaches turn
     Before the fire, but let it burn,
     Both sides and haunches, till the whole
     Converted be into one coal!

  Cla. What devil's pater-noster mumbles she?

Alk. Stay, you will hear more of her witchery.

The Second Charm.

Maud. The swilland dropsy enter in
　　　　The lazy cuke, and swell his skin,
　　　　And the old mormal on his shin
　　　　Now prick and itch withouten blin!
Cla. Speak out, hag! We may hear your devil's
　　matins.

The Third Charm.

Maud. The pain we call St Anton's fire,
　　　　The gout, or what we can desire
　　　　To cramp a cuke in every limb,
　　　　Before they dine yet, seize on him!

Alk. A foul ill spirit hath possessed her.
Am. O Karol, Karol! call him back again!
Lio. Her thoughts do work upon her in her slumber,
And may express some part of her disease.
　Rob. Observe and mark, but trouble not her ease.
　Am. Oh, Oh!
Mar.　　　How is't, Amie?
Mel.　　　　　　　　Wherefore start you?
　Am. O Karol, he is fair and sweet!
Maud.　　　　　　　　What then,
Are there not flowers as sweet and fair as men?
The lily is fair, and rose is sweet.
　Am.　　　　　　　Ay, so:
Let all the roses and the lilies go;
Karol is only fair to me.
　Mar.　　　　　And why?
　Am. Alas! For Karol, Marian, I could die;
Karol, he singeth sweetly too!

Maud.   What then,
Are there not birds sing sweeter far than men?
   Am. I grant the linnet, lark, and bullfinch sing,
But best the dear good angel of the spring,
The nightingale.
   Maud.   Then why, then why alone
Should his notes please you?
   Am.   I not long agone
Took a delight with wanton kids to play,
And sport with little lambs a summer's day,
And view their frisks; methought it was a sight
Of joy to see my two brave rams to fight!
Now Karol only all delight doth move,
All that is Karol, Karol, I approve.
This very morning but I did bestow
(It was a little gainst my will, I know)
A single kiss upon the silly swain,
And now I wish that very kiss again.
His lip is softer, sweeter, than the rose;
His mouth and tongue with dropping honey flows.
The relish of it was a pleasing thing.
   Maud. Yet like the bees it had a little sting.
   Am. And sunk, and sticks yet in my marrow
      deep,
And what doth hurt me I now wish to keep.
   Mar. Alas, how innocent her story is!
   Am. I do remember, Marian, I have oft
With pleasure kiss'd my lambs and puppies soft,
And once a dainty fine roe fawn I had,
Of whose out-skipping bounds I was as glad
As of my health, and him I oft would kiss;
Yet had his no such sting or pain as this;
They never prick'd or hurt my heart. And, for

They were so blunt and dull, I wish no more.
But this that hurts and pricks doth please; this sweet
Mingled with sour I wish again to meet;
And that delay methinks most tedious is
That keeps or hinders me of Karol's kiss.

    Mar. We'll send for him, sweet Amie, to come to
       you.

    Maud. But I will keep him off, if charms will do it.
                     [She goes murmuring out.

    Cla. Do you mark the murmuring hag, how she
       doth mutter?

    Rob. I like her not... and less her manners now.

    Alk. She is a shrewd, deformed piece, I vow.

    Lio. As crooked as her body.

    Rob.   I believe
She can take any shape, as Scathlock says.

    Alk. She may deceive the sense, but really
She cannot change herself.

    Rob.   Would I could see her
Once more in Marian's form! for I am certain
Now, it was she abus'd us, as I think
My Marian and my love now innocent;
Which faith I seal unto her with this kiss,
And call you all to witness of my penance.

    Alk. It was believ'd before, but now confirm'd,
That we have seen the monster.

Scene VII

To them *Tuck, John, Much, Scarlet.*

Tuck.   Hear you how
Poor Tom, the cook, is taken? All his joints
Do crack as if his limbs were tied with points,
His whole frame slackens, and a kind of rack
Runs down along the spondyls of his back;
A gout or cramp now seizeth on his head,
Then falls into his feet; his knees are lead;
And he can stir his either hand no more
Than a dead stump to his office, as before.

   Alk. He is bewitch'd.

   Cla.   This is an argument
Both of her malice and her power, we see.

   Alk. She must by some device restrained be,
Or she'll go far in mischief.

   Rob.   Advise how,
Sage shepherd; we shall put it straight in practice.

   Alk. Send forth your woodmen then into the walks,
Or let them prick her footing hence; a witch
Is sure a creature of melancholy,
And will be found or sitting in her form
Or else at relief, like a hare.

   Cla.   You speak,
Alken, as if you knew the sport of witch-hunting,
Or starting of a hag.

   [*enter George to the huntsmen, who by themselves*
   continue the scene, the rest going off.

   Rob.   Go, sirs, about it.
Take George here with you; he can help to find her.
Leave Tuck and Much behind to dress the dinner
In the cook's stead.

Muc.   We'll care to get that done.

Rob. Come, Marian, let's withdraw into the bower.

Scene VIII

John, Scarlet, Scathlock, George.

John. Rare sport, I swear, this hunting of the witch
Will make us!

Scar.   Let's advise upon't, like huntsmen.

Geo. An we can spy her once, she is our own.

Scar. First think which way she formeth, on what
        wind,
Or north or south.

Geo.   For, as the shepherd said,
A witch is a kind of hare.

Scat.   And marks the weather
As the hare does.

John.   Where shall we hope to find her?

                                    [*Alken returns.*

Alk. I have ask'd leave to assist you, jolly huntsmen,
If an old shepherd may be heard among you,
Not jeer'd or laugh'd at.

John.   Father, you will see
Robin Hood's household know more courtesy.

Scat. Who scorns at eld peels off his own young
        hairs.

Alk. Ye say right well. Know ye the witch's dell?

Scar. No more than I do know the walks of hell.

Alk. Within a gloomy dimble she doth dwell,
Down in a pit o'ergrown with brakes and briars,
Close by the ruins of a shaken abbey
Torn with an earthquake down unto the ground,
'Mongst graves and grots, near an old charnel-house;

Where you shall find her sitting in her form,
As fearful and melancholic as that
She is about, with caterpillars' kells
And knotty cobwebs rounded in with spells.
Thence she steals forth to relief in the fogs
And rotten mists, upon the fens and bogs,
Down to the drowned lands of Lincolnshire;
To make ewes cast their lambs, swine eat their farrow,
The housewife's tun not work, nor the milk churn;
Writhe children's wrists, and suck their breath in sleep,
Get vials of their blood; and where the sea
Casts up his slimy ooze, search for a weed
To open locks with, and to rivet charms
Planted about her, in the wicked feat
Of all her mischiefs, which are manifold.

   John. I wonder such a story could be told
Of her dire deeds.
   Geo.   I thought a witch's banks
Had enclos'd nothing but the merry pranks
Of some old woman.
   Scar.   Yes, her malice more.
   Scat. As it would quickly appear, had we the store
Of his collects.
   Geo.   Ay, this gud learned man
Can speak her right.
   Scar.   He knows her shifts and haunts.
   Alk. And all her wiles and turns; the venom'd
      plants
Wherewith she kills; where the sad mandrake grows,
Whose groans are deathful; the dead-numbing night-
      shade,
The stupifying hemlock, adder's tongue,
And martagon; the shrieks of luckless owls

We hear, and croaking night-crows in the air;
Green-bellied snakes, blue fire-drakes in the sky,
And giddy flitter-mice with leather wings;
The scaly beetles with their haubergeons
That make a humming murmur as they fly.
There in the stocks of trees white fays do dwell,
And span-long elves that dance about a pool
With each a little changeling in their arms;
The airy spirits play with falling stars,
And mount the sphere of fire to kiss the moon;
While she sits reading by the glow-worm's light,
Or rotten wood, o'er which the worm hath crept,
The baneful schedule of her nocent charms,
And binding characters through which she wounds
Her puppets, the sigilla of her witchcraft.
All this I know, and I will find her for you,
And show you her sitting in her form; I'll lay
My hand upon her, make her throw her scut
Along her back, when she doth start before us.
But you must give her law, and you shall see her
Make twenty leaps and doubles, cross the paths,
And then squat down beside us.

   John.   Crafty crone!
I long to be at the sport, and to report it.

   Scar. We'll make this hunting of the witch as
       famous
As any other blast of venery.

   Scat. Hang her, foul hag! She'll be a stinking
       chase:
I had rather have the hunting of her heir.

   Geo. If we could come to see her, cry *So haw!* once.

   Alk. That I do promise, or I'm no good hag-finder.
                                  [exeunt.

ACT III

Scene I

Puck Hairy.

The fiend hath much to do that keeps a school,
Or is the father of a family,
Or governs but a country academy;
His labours must be great, as are his cares,
To watch all turns, and cast how to prevent them.
This dame of mine here, Maud, grows high in evil,
And thinks she does all, when 'tis I, her devil,
That both delude her, and must yet protect her;
She's confident in mischief, and presumes
The changing of her shape will still secure her.
But that may fail, and divers hazards meet
Of other consequence, which I must look to,
Not let her be surpris'd on the first catch.
I must go dance about the forest now,
And firk it like a goblin, till I find her.
Then will my service come worth acceptation
When not expected of her, when the help
Meets the necessity, and both do kiss:
'Tis call'd the timing of a duty, this.

[*exit.*

Scene II

Karol, Douce.

Kar. Sure, you are very like her: I conceiv'd
You had been she, seeing you run afore me;
For such a suit she made her gainst this feast,
In all resemblance, or the very same
(I saw her in it); had she liv'd to enjoy it,

She had been there an acceptable guest
To Marian and the gentle Robin Hood,
Who are the crown and garland of the wood.
 Dou. I cannot tell; my mother gave it me,
And bad me wear it.
 Kar.   Who? The wise good woman,
Old Maud of Papplewick?
 Dou. Yes. [*Aeglamour enters.*] This sullen man!
I cannot like him; I must take my leave.
            [*Douce goes out.*

 Aeg. What said she to you?
 Kar.   Who?
 Aeg.   Earine:
I saw her talking with you, or her ghost;
For she indeed is drown'd in old Trent's bottom.
Did she not tell who would have pull'd her in,
And had her maidenhead upon the place,
The river's brim, the margin of the flood?
No ground is holy enough (you know my meaning);
Lust is committed in king's palaces,
And yet their majesties not violated.
No words!
 Kar. How sad and wild his thoughts are! Gone?
     [*Aeglamour goes out, but comes in again.*
 Aeg. But she, as chaste as was her name, Earine,
Died undeflower'd, and now her sweet soul hovers
Here in the air above us, and doth haste
To get up to the moon and Mercury,
And whisper Venus in her orb; then spring
Up to old Saturn, and come down by Mars,
Consulting Jupiter, and seat herself
Just in the midst with Phoebus, temp'ring all
The jarring spheres, and giving to the world

Again his first and tuneful planeting.
Oh, what an age will here be of new concords,
Delightful harmony, to rock old sages,
Twice infants, in the cradle o' speculation,
And throw a silence upon all the creatures!

> [*He goes out again, but returns as soon as before.*

Kar. A cogitation of the highest rapture!

Aeg. The loudest seas and most enraged winds
Shall lose their clangour; tempest shall grow hoarse,
Loud thunder dumb, and every spece of storm
Laid in the lap of listening nature, hush'd,
To hear the changed chime of this eighth sphere.
Take tent and hearken for it; lose it not.

> [*Aeglamour departs.*

Scene III

Clarion, Lionel, Karol.

Cla. Oh, here is Karol! Was not that the sad
Shepherd slipp'd from him?

Lio.   Yes, I guess it was.
Who was that left you, Karol?

Kar.   The last man!
Whom we shall never see himself again,
Or ours, I fear; he starts away from hand so,
And all the touches or soft stroke of reason
Ye can apply; no colt is so unbroken,
Or hawk yet half so haggard or unmann'd.
He takes all toys that his wild fancy proffers,
And flies away with them. He now conceives
That my lost sister, his Earine,
Is lately turn'd a sphere amid the seven,
And reads a music-lecture to the planets;
And with this thought he's run to call them hearers.

Cla. Alas, this is a strain'd but innocent fancy!
I'll follow him and find him if I can.
Meantime go you with Lionel, sweet Karol;
He will acquaint you with an accident
Which much desires your presence on the place.
                                        [*exit Clarion.*

Scene IV

Karol, Lionel.

Kar. What is it, Lionel, wherein I may serve you?
Why do you so survey and circumscribe me,
As if you stuck one eye into my breast,
And with the other took my whole dimensions?
   Lio. I wish you had a window in your bosom
Or in your back, I might look thorough you,
And see your in-parts, Karol,—liver, heart,—
For there the seat of love is; whence the boy,
The winged archer, hath shot home a shaft
Into my sister's breast, the innocent Amie,
Who now cries out upon her bed on Karol,
Sweet-singing Karol, the delicious Karol,
That kiss'd her like a Cupid! In your eyes
She says his stand is, and between your lips
He runs forth his divisions to her ears,
But will not bide there 'less yourself do bring him.
Go with me, Karol, and bestow a visit
In charity upon the afflicted maid,
Who pineth with the languor of your love.
   [*To them Maudlin and Douce, but Maudlin appearing
   like Marian.*
   Maud. Whither intend you? Amie is recover'd,
Feels no such grief as she complain'd of lately;

This maiden hath been with her from her mother,
Maudlin, the cunning woman, who hath sent her
Herbs for her head, and simples of that nature
Have wrought upon her a miraculous cure,
Settled her brain to all our wish and wonder.
 Lio. So instantly? You know I now but left her
Possess'd with such a fit almost to a frenzy,
Yourself, too, fear'd her, Marian, and did urge
My haste to seek out Karol, and to bring him
 Maud. I did so. But the skill of that wise woman
And her great charity of doing good
Hath by the ready hand of this deft lass,
Her daughter, wrought effects beyond belief
And to astonishment; we can but thank,
And praise, and be amazed, while we tell it.
[They go out.
 Lio. 'Tis strange that any art should so help nature
In her extremes.
 Kar.   Then it appears most real
When th'other is deficient.
[enter Robin Hood.
 Rob.   Wherefore stay you
Discoursing here, and haste not with your succours
To poor afflicted Amie, that so needs them?
 Lio. She is recover'd well: your Marian told us
But now here. [*Enter Maudlin like Marian.*] See, she
  is return'd to affirm it!
 Rob. My Marian!
 Maud.   Robin Hood! Is he here?
  [*Maudlin espying Robin Hood would run out, but
  he stays her by the girdle and runs in with her.
  He returns with the girdle broken, and she in her
  own shape.*

Rob.   Stay!
What was't you ha' told my friend?
  Maud.   Help! murder! help!
You will not rob me, outlaw? Thief, restore
My belt that ye have broken!
  Rob.   Yes. Come near.
  Maud. Not in your gripe.
  Rob.   Was this the charmed circle,
The copy that so cozen'd and deceiv'd us?
I'll carry hence the trophy of your spoils;
My men shall hunt you, too, upon the start,
And course you soundly.
  Maud.   I shall make them sport,
And send some home without their legs or arms;
I'll teach them to climb stiles, leap ditches, ponds,
And lie i' the waters, if they follow me!
  Rob. Out, murmuring hag!
                [exeunt Robin Hood, Karol, and Lionel.

SCENE V

Maudlin.

                    I must use all my powers,
Lay all my wits to piecing of this loss;
Things run unluckily. Where's my Puck Hairy?
Hath he forsook me?   *[enter Puck Hairy.*
  Puck.   At your beck, madam.
  Maud. Oh, Puck, my goblin, I have lost my belt;
The strong thief, Robin Outlaw, forc'd it from me!
  Puck. They are other clouds, and blacker, threat
          you, dame;
You must be wary, and pull in your sails,
And yield unto the weather of the tempest.

You think your power's infinite as your malice,
And would do all your anger prompts you to;
But you must wait occasions, and obey them;
Sail in an egg-shell, make a straw your mast,
A cobweb all your cloth, and pass unseen
Till you have scap'd the rocks that are about you.
   Maud. What rocks about me?
   Puck.   I do love, madam,
To show you all your dangers when you are past them.
Come, follow me; I'll once more be your pilot,
And you shall thank me.
   Maud.   Lucky, my lov'd goblin!
                             [Lorell meets her.
Where are you gaand now?
   Lor.   Unto my tree,
To see my maistress.
   Maud.   Gang thy gait, and try
Thy turns with better luck, or hang thysell!...

THE ARGUMENT OF THE REST OF THE
THIRD ACT

Amie is gladded with the sight of Karol, &c. In the meantime enters Lorell with purpose to ravish Earine, and calling her forth to that lewd end he by the hearing of Clarion's footing is stayed, and forced to commit her hastily to the tree again; where Clarion coming by and hearing a voice singing draws near unto it; but Aeglamour hearing it also and knowing it to be Earine's falls into a superstitious commendation of it as being an angel's, and in the air; when Clarion espies a hand put forth from the tree and makes towards it, leaving Aeglamour to his wild fancy, who quitteth the place; and Clarion beginning to court the hand and make love to it, there ariseth a mist suddenly, which darkening all the place Clarion loseth himself and the tree where Earine is enclosed, lamenting his misfortune, with the unknown nymph's misery. The air clearing, enters the witch with her son and daughter, tells them how she had caused that late darkness, to free Lorell from surprisal and his prey from being rescued from him, bids him look to her and lock her up more carefully, and follow her to assist a work she hath in hand, of recovering her lost girdle, which she laments the loss of with cursings, execrations, wishing confusion to their feast and meeting; sends her son and daughter to gather certain simples for her purpose and bring them to her dell. This Puck hearing prevents, and shews her error still. The huntsmen having found her footing follow the track and prick after her. She gets to her dell and takes her form. Enter; Alken has spied her sitting with her spindle, threads, and images.

They are eager to seize her presently, but Alken persuades them to let her begin her charms, which they do. Her son and daughter come to her; the huntsmen are affrighted as they see her work go forward; and, over-hasty to apprehend her, she escapeth them all, by the help and delusions of Puck.

THE END OF THE THIRD ACT.

TEXTUAL NOTES

P. 2. (also called *Karol*): *not in* 1641.

P. 5, l. 17. Whether: *pronounced* Where, *and so spelt* 1641.

P. 10, l. 22. her: 1641 their

P. 14, l. 23. stream: 1641 streames

P. 15, l. 29. Smite: 1641 Snite

P. 17, l. 15. Look: 1641 Lookes

P. 18, l. 3. *Lio.*: 1641, *probably by Jonson's inadvertence*, Kar. *It does not much matter who is substituted for Karolin.*

P. 18, l. 17. caul: 1641 call'd

P. 19, l. 16. *Scar.*: 1641 *Sca.*

P. 28, l. 20. With all the barkand: 1641 Withall the barke and

P. 39, l. 6 *Scar.*: 1641 *Sca.*

P. 40, l. 20. *Scat.*: 1641 *Sca.*

P. 47. Scene V: *in* 1641 *this scene begins after* Where's my Puck Hairy?

P. 48, l. 11. gaand: 1641 gaang

CAMBRIDGE
PLAIN TEXTS

The following Volumes are the latest
additions to this Series:

English

JONSON. The Sad Shepherd.
With a Note by L. J. Potts. 1s. 3d.

HENRYSON. The Testament of Cresseid.
With a Note by A. L. Attwater. 1s. 3d.

GOWER. Selections from Confessio Amantis.
With a Note by H. S. Bennett. 1s. 3d.

French

MOLIÈRE: La Critique de l'École des Femmes
and L'Impromptu de Versailles.
With a Note by A. Tilley. 1s. 3d.

German

HOFFMANN: Der Kampf der Sänger.
With a Note by G. Waterhouse. 1s. 6d.

LESSING: Hamburgische Dramaturgie I, II.
With a Note by G. Waterhouse. 1s. 6d. each

Spanish

OLD SPANISH BALLADS.
With a Note by J. P. Howard. 1s. 6d.

VILLENA, LEBRIJA, ENCINA. Selections
With a Note by I. Bullock. 1s. 6d.

small octavo pages of text, preceded

note on the author

LIMP CLOTH

German

GRILLPARZER. Der Arme Spielmann. Erinnerungen an Beethoven.
HERDER. Kleinere Aufsätze I.
HOFFMANN. Der Kampf der Sänger.
LESSING. Hamburgische Dramaturgie I.
LESSING. Hamburgische Dramaturgie II.

Italian

ALFIERI. La Virtù Sconosciuta.
GOZZI, GASPARO. La Gazzetta Veneta.
LEOPARDI. Pensieri.
MAZZINI. Fede e Avvenire.
ROSMINI. Cinque Piaghe.

Spanish

BOLIVAR, SIMON. Address to the Venezuelan Congress at Angostura, February 15, 1819.
CALDERÓN. La Cena de Baltasar.
CERVANTES. Prologues and Epilogue.
CERVANTES. Rinconete y Cortadillo.
ESPRONCEDA. El Estudiante de Salamanca.
LOPE DE VEGA. El Mejor Alcalde. El Rey.
LUIS DE LEON. Poesías Originales.
OLD SPANISH BALLADS.
VILLEGAS. El Abencerraje.
VILLENA: LEBRIJA: ENCINA. Selections.

SOME PRESS OPINIONS

"These are delightful, slim little books....The print is very clear and pleasant to the eye....These Cambridge Plain Texts are just the kind of book that a lover of letters longs to put in his pocket as a prophylactic against boredom." THE NEW STATESMAN

"These little books....are exquisitely printed on excellent paper and are prefaced in each case by a brief biographical note concerning the author: otherwise entirely unencum‑bered with notes or explanatory matter, they form the most delicious and companionable little volumes we re‑member to have seen. The title‑page is a model of refined taste—*simplex munditiis*." THE ANGLO‑FRENCH REVIEW

"With their admirable print, the little books do credit to the great Press which is responsible for them." NOTES AND QUERIES

"The series of texts of notable Italian works which is being issued at Cambridge should be made known wherever there is a chance of studying the language; they are clear, in a handy form, and carefully edited....The venture deserves well of all who aim at the higher culture." THE INQUIRER

"Selections of this kind, made by competent hands, may serve to make us acquainted with much that we should otherwise miss. To read two of Donne's tremendous sermons may send many readers eagerly to enlarge their knowledge of one of the great glories of the English pulpit." THE HOLBORN REVIEW

"This new Spanish text‑book, printed on excellent paper, in delightfully clear type and of convenient pocket size, preserves the high level of achievement that characterises the series." THE TEACHER'S WORLD *on* "Cervantes: Prologues and Epilogue"

"It is difficult to praise too highly the Cambridge Plain Texts." THE LONDON MERCURY